Sound Between Matter and Spirit

SOUND BETWEEN MATTER AND SPIRIT

by

Frits H. Julius

Translated by
Gerhard Bedding

Mercury Press

Second printing: 2016

ISBN: 978-0-929979-33-5

Printed & Published in the USA by
MERCURY PRESS
Fellowship Community
241 Hungry Hollow Road
Chestnut Ridge, N.Y. 10977
www.mercurypress.org

Table of Contents

Introduction

Frederik "Frits" Hendrik Julius died on November 30, 1970, at the age of sixty-eight. For most of his life he was a science teacher at the Free School in The Hague, the first Waldorf school in the Netherlands. In his last few years Frits also inspired many older students at Emerson College in Forest Row, England, and at Waldorf teacher training institutes in Jarna, Sweden, and Stuttgart, Germany.

In his university training as a biologist, Frits experienced a mixture of hope and despair. He felt he was at the threshold of many mysteries and expected to be helped in crossing at least some of those thresholds. Somehow, this never happened. The analytical approach to the life sciences at the university had a deadening effect. In autobiographical notes Frits mentions that, toward the end of his botany studies, he felt so completely cut off from nature that he had no inner experiences when he looked at freshly sprouting plant life or blossoms. He noticed only malfunctions and disease.

From another biology student Frits heard about Rudolf Steiner. The first book he read, *Goethe's World View,* was a turning point in his life. One sentence hit him like a bolt of lightning: "For Goethe there is only one source of knowledge: the world of experience, in which the world of ideas is enclosed." Another major event that helped to launch Frits on his new Goethean journey was a chemistry course he took from Dr. Ehrenfried Pfeiffer.* Through life-long, disciplined self-training, Frits became an eminent nature observer and Goethean scientist.

In spite of his busy teaching career and chronic health problems, Frits Julius managed to write about a dozen books and some two hundred articles. A number of the books have been translated into English.

---

* See Alla Selawry, *Ehrenfried Pfeiffer: Pioneer of Spiritual Research and Practice.* Mercury Press, Spring Valley, N.Y., 1992.

My experience of sound, tone and music has been greatly deepened by Julius' *Sound Between Matter and Spirit.* I hope that this translation will bring such joy to many others.

I had the privilege of sharing one camping weekend, at the summer solstice of 1953, with Frits Julius and a few friends. We camped on the *Veluwe,* a large nature reservation in the Netherlands. After we rose early and experienced an exquisitely beautiful dawn and sunrise, Frits guided us to many special nooks and crannies with wonderful plant and animal phenomena that we would have never noticed without him. Through Frits' attitude and manner of speaking we felt that these things were sacred for him. People who observed Frits conducting demonstrations also sensed that the laboratory table was his altar. Another side of Frits came forward on our camping weekend – his very dry, down-to-earth sense of humor, a source of many laughs and chuckles.

Thank you, Frits Julius, for your gifts to all of us. Your spirit is very much alive!

Gerhard Bedding
Summer Solstice, 1992

1

Seeing and Hearing

We can best start the characterization of sound phenomena by comparing them with our visual experience. In seeing we usually direct our attention sharply toward the object. It is as if our innermost being reaches out towards it. The eye serves as a gate through which our soul enters the wide halls of light-filled space where it has many diverse encounters.

In listening, however, we open ourselves to what wants to enter us from our environment. Sound weaves around us; it is much less fixed to a specific place. Sound forces itself on us so that we have difficulty rejecting it. Sound often penetrates deeply into our organism, sometimes giving us pleasure and sometimes pain.

Color impressions also can affect our feelings, but we have to help this process by increasing our sensitivity. It is rather easy to withdraw from such a visual experience by closing our eyes or diverting our attention.

When one earnestly wants to develop a deeper connection with sound, the ear also can become a gate through which one enters a new world. This world has more of an inward quality and is less spatial than the world of light.

In seeing we can experience something akin to listening when we lie on our back on a beautiful summer day, gazing at the blue heavens over and around us. The front part of the eye, which is directed toward grasping and touching distinct forms, loses its hold. Just as with sound, we begin to swim in the impressions. When we become aware of this dimension, we can learn to practice such swimming by gazing with concentration at a large, even-colored surface. Ultimately we can also learn to achieve this experience by concentrating on small colored spots. Such a small spot, for example, a blue flower, is then used as the narrow mouth of a harbor through which we sail out on a sea of color.

In this way we can learn to exclude spatial relationships and to develop a wholly different side of seeing. Thus we are moving from the outer surface toward an inner world.

The best method for learning this art is to begin by practicing listening. The more one's perception begins to resemble inward listening, the greater the depths one can reach not only with the eye but also with the other senses. In our sense of hearing we possess a sublime instrument for practicing deep empathy toward another creature or even toward an object.

A well-illuminated object continually beams its image over all other things in its environment. Yes, it even calls forth these other things and makes them send out their own images. (The object reflects the light, as the physicist calls it.) Such images do not have distinct forms, but they carry the color tone of the object's substance; with this color they illuminate other things.

All sunlit space is full of the wonderful play of such images that are being sent back and forth. The style of this bouncing play is light and airy. It only takes place between the outer surfaces of things. We make use of this by painting things or, sometimes, ourselves. Usually the color reveals something of the character of an object, but what lies below the thin outer layer can have a wholly different quality.

What is expressed by a sound, however, comes from within the sound producer. A vase, which may seem perfect to the eye, betrays its hidden crack by the sound it makes. An animal's distress call comes from the depth of its inner being. The whole body, tense and cramped, takes part in such a call.

The whole world of color is in the first place a manifestation of light. The color of a substance points toward a special relation of that substance to the light. In the world of sound, however, the sound-producing object or the complaining animal expresses itself. Though the sound may have been generated by an action from the outside, the object that is struck expresses its own nature. It would be impossible to speak of the "deeds and sufferings of sound" *(Taten und Leiden des Klanges)* as Goethe spoke of the "deeds and sufferings of light" *(Taten und Leiden des Lichtes).*

2

Sound as Expression of the Essence of Things

An object that is struck produces a sound. The quality of this sound depends for a large part on accidental circumstances: the nature of the blow, the material used, etc. But one can always find something of the essence of the object in the sound it makes.

The sounds made by an animal are much less accidental. Even though they may come from physical mechanisms that are much like the sounding objects mentioned above, the sounds express something of the animal's inner nature. They are not just the sounds of two dead objects hitting or rubbing each other.

This is also true of the human being. He may shout with joy, purr with satisfaction or cry out in fear or pain. Much of the animal's inner life is a reaction to outside stimuli. Man is only truly human when he is not subject to accidental circumstances, when he expresses his own being as well as the essence of the things around him.

Man has the gift of speech; he commands words. This means that he is called upon to lend his voice not only to his own emotions but to all things and creatures and thus reveal their hidden nature. Through his senses, man receives fragmentary expressions of the essence of a thing or creature; by using words and names he tries to express that essence more fully.

Why are many names often used only for one thing or creature? No single thing or living creature embodies the perfect image of the eternal archetype. Even the most developed creatures are more or less distorted by impediments that obscure a full revelation of their essence. This also applies to the name that a certain language may give to an object or creature. It is apt to reveal only one or a few aspects of its essence. If this were not so, each creature or thing would have only one name, not many. Yet the giving of a name is an endeavor to approach the essence of a thing or being as closely as possible.

3

Sound, Tone and Speech

There are many kinds of sounds. Even air in motion can be heard. It may whisper softly or scream and whistle along the things that surround us. The power of the heavens may reveal itself in the mighty rolls and claps of thunder.

We only have to think of water and we can already hear the spattering rain, the babbling brook, the roaring surf. Solid objects can be tapped, rattled, rubbed, ground, etc.

When we search for the deeper significance of all these sounds, we are at first confronted with a formless mass of various qualities. In this chaos we find sounds so clear and formed that they are like crystals within an opaque mass of rocks. These are the tones which distinguish themselves by clarity, order and purity. Thus they can become one of the windows through which we can look into the secret room of sound.

A fully-formed crystal is an exception in the world of minerals. Similarly, there are only a few tones in the vast multitude of sounds. Yet, these tones occur in all realms of nature. There are caves where the stalactites have such a miraculous form that they sound like a bell when struck. Among the birds we find something of a still higher order. They produce tones so manifold, pure and refined that the human listener can be touched in the core of his being.

Though bird song stems from a most noble realm of creation, the human being can still reach higher. He can give different qualities to a tone. He can tune notes in a pure or dissonant relation. He can build waves in his sequences of notes. Thus he can bring form into the sequence of time.

In bird song one can hear something that reaches beyond the soul condition of a single animal. Wondrous secrets of nature sound from the throats of birds. Man surpasses the bird in his ability to sing his own joy or sorrow. What is more, he can open himself to the moods of another soul and express these moods. Yes, man even tries to give voice to the spirit-ground of the world.

With his singing, especially with choral singing, man reaches far into the realms of soul and spirit. Yet, with the word, a gift which he alone possesses, he can still reach higher. A rich variety of sound qualities and forms, fused into a single, pithy phrase, can become a wide-open gate to realms of soul and spirit. The most obvious aspects, as well as the hidden essence of a thing, can thus be expressed.

In the vowels we find something akin to musical sounds. They arise only from the inner life of ensouled beings. They are accompanied by consonants, the imitators of the sounds and gestures of events in nature. The consonants give the word its sharp outline.

Not only with his own organism can man produce sounds. As spirit-bearer he is able to penetrate into the secrets of sound in such a way that he can mold dead matter into musical instruments. He gives them a form in which heavenly harmony and order are expressed. Thus he makes even the world around him permeable for that higher purity that can be approached only by inner listening.

4

Pitch in Relation to the Character of the Sound Maker

Tone has three main aspects: pitch, quality and volume. Volume is not very important with regard to the essence of a tone. Quality will be discussed later.

Even rather undetermined sound in nature can be said to have a certain pitch. Only with real tones, of course, is the pitch sharply determined. The picture of a crystal, embedded in a more formless mass of minerals, is useful as a comparison. The tone is the simplest, most strictly built, most lawful, among all sound phenomena. In comparison, all other sounds seem to be a fragmentary, splintered mass.

Low-pitched sounds are heard in natural events in which gigantic masses play a role: thunder, heavy breakers against the rocky shore, an avalanche of boulders. A high-pitched tone is produced where small particles move or bump: the babbling of a little waterfall in a brook, the soft tinkling shells at the beach which are moved back and forth by the surf.

A rather low tone is heard when one taps a piece of furniture or a wall with a large, not-too-hard object. If one takes increasingly smaller and harder objects, and if one also taps more vigorously, the same wall or piece of furniture will produce increasingly higher sounds. Animals that are large, such as the lion, rhinoceros or cow, express themselves with low-pitched sounds.

High tones are produced by small or delicate animals such as many rodents or lap dogs. Generally, animals which have overcome heaviness in their structure and way of life such as birds express themselves in high-pitched tones. It is interesting to note that bats, which as mammals should be earth-bound, produce tones of such a high pitch that they lie beyond the hearing range of many persons.

Man can imitate a cow. He can produce low sounds that arise from the depths of his body; he can also try to imitate a bird and then experiences that this can only be done with high head-sounds. Indeed, our head has something in common with the birds: it is sharply formed and we carry it without experiencing its heaviness. In contrast, our lower body is like a cow: clumsy, unformed and subject to gravity We can approximate the roar of a lion in the middle region of our body by using our lungs to their full extent and volume.

Children and young animals express themselves in high-pitched sounds. When they grow up and connect themselves more deeply with matter, they produce deeper sounds. The male has a deeper voice than the female and thus he shows a deeper penetration into the world of matter during his development. When fully rested or relaxed, a human being tends to produce low sounds. This is also generally true for animals. Shortly after awakening our sounds are remarkably low-pitched. This is generally the case when there is little tension in relation to the environment. This can occur when there is real harmony or contentment as well as when one is forced to submit to superior forces. When a person is forced to feel resigned to his fate, he will speak in low tones. Submissiveness expresses itself in deep sounds.

Excitement sharply raises the voices of humans as well as of the animals. Especially striking are the two registers of the pig. The blackbird's cry of alarm becomes higher when danger is near. One finds similar differences in the sounds human beings produce. A person can scream with excitement. Generally, one can say that a creature in a state of excitement shows tension and great activity in relation to the environment. Low-pitched sounds are connected with mass and heaviness, with the depth of the world. Also, they may express sluggishness or a state of rest and relaxation. High-pitched sounds occur where mass plays no role or is overcome by a connection with the heights of the world. Also, high-pitched sounds often express violent activity and mobility.

5

About the Nature of High and Low Tones

High tones give us an impression of clarity and cheerfulness when their sound is mild, transparent and not screeching or raucous. One could even say that they have a radiating quality similar to light. Our sense of hearing seems to tell us that such sounds have no heaviness, no gravity.

When we play a scale, starting with the low tones, we feel ourselves carried upward. The word "scale" (Dutch: "tone ladder") expresses well what we experience. In our body we can find the tone ladder in a physical form. When we sing a scale, we can feel the place from which each tone sounds in an ascending order: from deep in our lungs, or even our abdomen, to up in or above our head. The low tones give us a dull, dark impression. Sometimes they may sound very gloomy. Their quality is heavy and earthy compared with the high tones. In the low tones we hear the depths of the world, in the high tones the heights of heaven.

6

Pitch of a String

Much of what we discussed about pitch in general can be illustrated with a single string by changing its condition: more or less tension, shortening or lengthening, or taking a thicker or thinner string. A loose string of a violin does not have much character; it yields to all kinds of influences and does not maintain a clear form. The sounds it may make depend mainly on what is done to it, not on its own essence.

Now we slowly put it under tension. Soon it begins to show a definite form and begins to maintain itself against outside influences. The more one increases the tension, the more character the string acquires. Increasingly it resists any change in its form. Now it produces a real tone which becomes higher and more and more transparent as the tension increases.

With the low tones the string still made a heavy impression; it could be seen yielding to pressure. With the high tones the tautness of the string gives us a glass-like, brittle impression when we touch it.

Besides increasing the tension one can also raise the pitch by shortening the string. The same result can be obtained by lightening the string, by taking away some of its mass, leaving tension and length unchanged.

The tone can be lowered by relaxing the tension, by lengthening the string and by making it heavier. The latter can be achieved, for instance, by winding a metal thread around those strings which have to produce a low tone.

It is as if there are two parties battling for the pitch on one side tension, shortness and lightness, on the other side slackness, greater length, heaviness. Increasing length or thickness has the same result: more mass, more matter. Decreasing length or thickness has the opposite result.

There are actually only two principles that are clearly opposed: the tension that makes it possible for the string to maintain its form (which I propose to call *formative* force) stands opposite to the mass.

7

Nature of String Movements

What is the real difference between a taut and a slack string? In a slack string the cohesion of its parts is rather limited: one can move one side without noticeable effect on the other side. As soon as the string is taut it acts as one unit. If one pushes against such a string, it resists. It tries to regain its former shape with a sharp and immediate motion as soon as it is released. With increasing speed it approaches its old position. At the former position of rest the string now reaches its maximum speed, consequently overshooting its goal. We have a new phenomenon – motion. Through motion, the mass of the string has acquired a certain power: the principle of inertia demonstrates itself. This principle says that there always exists a resistance against every change in the condition of motion. If a body is at rest, it resists being put into motion; if it is moving, it resists acceleration or deceleration as well as change of direction. By pushing and releasing the quiet string, we have caused a rapid motion.

Now the motion exists and inertia tends to maintain it: each overshooting of the rest position produces resistance of the formative force of the string. This force increases and the motion decreases when the string approaches its maximal deflection. The motion stops completely and the tension is at its highest at the point of maximal deflection. The formative force now causes the return motion opposed by inertia. A gradual acceleration is the result until we have maximal motion and minimal tension in the center position.

The mass duly tends to maintain the motion of the body without regard for the totality of the string. On the other hand, the tension – the formative force – would like to keep the string only in its central position, resisting any influence from the environment. By its tension the string becomes as it were individualized, separated, freed, from its environment. It is interesting to imagine a condition in which the influence of the environment, and consequently inertia, would not exist. The string then would jump back immediately, with boundless speed, to its condition of rest.

By allowing a string to move freely, therefore, one brings into existence a rapid back and forth motion with sharply defined changes in speed and direction. One calls this phenomenon *vibration*. It is important to keep in mind that this peculiar phenomenon wholly belongs in the realm of rhythm.

Rhythm can only occur where an interplay exists between two forces of opposite polarities.

In the case of our string, these forces are brought into play by our starting motion. The resulting rhythm is a third force. It has a strict and unassailable quality.

This shows itself with the string, for instance, in that the frequency of the rhythm, measured by the number of back and forth motions in a certain unit of time, is independent of the magnitude of the deflection from the rest position (the amplitude). The amplitude of a vibrating string slowly decreases; the tone becomes softer and finally falls below our hearing range. Shortly thereafter the string comes to a complete rest. All this time the rhythm, as well as the pitch, has been constant.

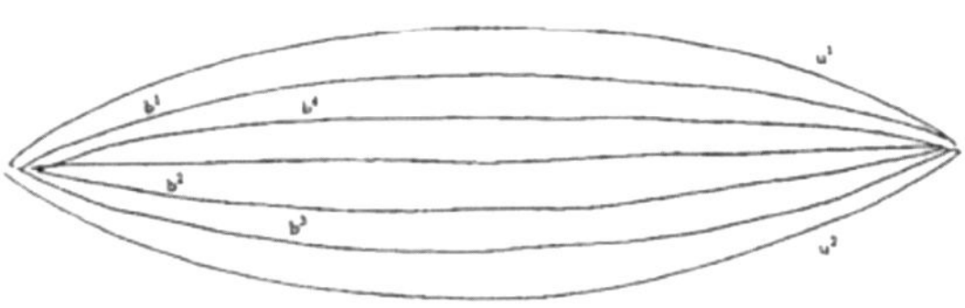

Vibrating Sting
Figure 1

Though rhythm can be sharply defined, it does not belong to the world of matter, in contrast to the formative force and the mass. Its laws place it one level higher than the forces between which it intermediates. Spatially it can show great variations, but it obeys rigid laws in the realm of time. A vibration rhythm occurs on the basis of an interplay between two spatial forces. However, it opens itself to the extra-spatial world. One might say that rhythm creates in the spatial world an opening with suction power, thus inviting sound from a realm outside our physical senses.

As we have noticed before, sound is deeply related to the essence of things. Now we see how it is possible that in sound something can live which is not spatial.

8

Sound Production in General

What we have found with the string also applies to general sound phenomena. Sound only occurs where matter exists in a certain form and when this form is attacked.

When the form is changeable – not clearly defined – the sound will also have an undefined quality. When the form is sharply defined and constant, a well-defined and constant tone will result.

Sound is always an expression of movement and struggle. The mass in all sound producers almost always acts in the same way. The formative force can have very different qualities. When sound is made by a glass or a bell, the solidity of the materials – one might also say the elasticity – serves as a formative force. When a sound is made by a cylinder of air in a flute, the form of that air body is maintained by the solid tube. The resistance against form change, in this case, is also the result of the air's tendency to equalize any local change in pressure.

Everywhere and always the tone is based in the first place on rhythm and not only on mass and formative force. Bodies of equal weight do not always produce tones of equal pitch. This is also true of strings with equal tension. The pitch depends on both mass and formative force. It is the relation between the two that counts.

A certain pitch is always the result of the same proportion of formative force and mass. The harder, the tenser, but also the lighter and smaller a certain body is, the more it tends to produce high tones. The softer and slacker, but also the heavier and larger a body is, the more it tends toward the low tones.

High tones occur with bodies that sharply resist the environment, bodies that isolate themselves clearly. Low tones seem related to a tendency in a body to communicate with the environment. At least, one can say that bodies with low tones have less of a tendency to separate and isolate themselves.

When high tones and a strong formative force occur, a body is resisting an attack with a very sharp tendency to restore its form. The speed of the vibrating movement is high and the body will vibrate with a fast rhythm.

When the mass of a body becomes a significant factor, the less influential formative force needs much more time to restore the form: the movement becomes slow, the rhythm slack. It is clear that this must introduce something earthy and heavy into the quality of the accompanying tones. In the case of high tones, the fast victory of the formative force – the easy and, one might say, playful maintenance of form – will lend a clear, transparent, and joyful quality to the high tones.

9

Resounding and Resonance

There is a general tendency in a sound-producing body to transplant its sound into the environment or to take along the environment into the making of sound. This phenomenon has extraordinary significance.

In the animal world we find a very active answering that could be compared to resounding. Often, the cry of one member of a species calls forth the cries of the others. In farming country one has only to crow like a cock, late in the evening, to immediately elicit answers from all sides.

A tuning fork that is struck is only scarcely audible. However, if one puts it on another solid body, it makes that body resound and the tone is greatly amplified. A vibrating string also would be barely audible if it did not bring the violin's body into motion. Even the so-called transmission of sound – to be discussed later – is based on a similar principle.

Much more mysterious is the phenomenon of true resonance. For instance, one can open a piano, release the sound dampers and then sing into it a certain tone or a chord with the help of other voices. When the singing is silenced, the same tones that were sung can be heard from the strings in magically pure sounds. One can also strike a tuning fork and hold it over a bottle which is carefully tuned to it by filling it with a certain quantity of water. The air space in the bottle will also answer with a mysterious free-floating tone that far surpasses the volume of the fork.

That our mouth cavity was destined to be a resonator can be easily shown by holding a vibrating tuning fork in front of the slightly opened lips and then adjusting the shape of the mouth until it begins to resonate.

One feels here that something very mysterious is called forth that is inherent in the resonating space or object. This body or space only resonates if it can produce a tone of the same pitch as the sound producer, either as basic tone or as overtone. It is as if each body which can express itself in tones, listens and begins to sing as soon as it feels its essence touched. In mechanical terms one says that the resonating body begins to vibrate with the same frequency as the sound producer.

In the inner ear, in the cochlea, is a membrane of which it is assumed (Helmholtz) that specific places are activated by certain pitches. Our ability to discern pitch seems to be based on discerning these different locations. Our ability to hear then is partly based on resonance phenomena. And indeed, we feel as if listening means that we allow the re-sounding of what we have heard.

The phenomenon that we mentioned before, namely the feeling that the tones we sing resound in different parts of the body, depending on the pitch, belongs to this same area of resonance. The tone is propagated mainly by the vocal cords; the area of our body to which it is related makes it resound so that it receives the force to be carried far into the environment.

In this example we touch the real nature of sound. Sound has a contagious nature; it sets things in motion and even forms them. The contagious nature of sound can be noticed in many simple, everyday occurrences. It happens in the highest degree only to objects which have a delicately tuned relation to the sound producer – in other words, to those objects in which the same proportion exists between formative force and mass.

10

Echo

It can happen that we walk somewhere in nature, singing cheerfully, and suddenly we notice that our song is mixed with another that resembles it in every detail. We stop and listen – everything is silent. We call. Immediately our call is returned. Every tone, rhythm, yes, every little detail, is reproduced exactly, though, as it seems, somewhat ennobled. Now we are looking for a being that is able to do this, but we find nothing – nothing but a barren mountain wall or the edge of a forest.

The same thing can be experienced by calling into a deep well. It is as if every well harbors a slumbering voice with a miraculous ability to imitate.

If one searches where this echo phenomenon occurs, one soon makes the observation that it only occurs where the air space has a more or less solid wall that is hard to penetrate. Such a wall is by itself unable to serve as a sound producer and yet it can play the role of producer perfectly. When it does so, it does not only reproduce certain preferred, selected tones, as is the case with resonance. All tones, all sounds that we make, are heard again. There is no continuing sound as with resonance. For that, the ability to produce sound independently is necessary. No, everything is imitated in pure form, in the exact time sequence. The echo phenomenon can be noticed anywhere, any moment. In every wall of every house slumbers an echo. On a quiet evening, when one is the only one walking a wide city street, one hears the echo bouncing back from the other side of the street with each step.

It is also interesting to analyze the sound one can hear when bicycling on asphalt pavement. When one ascends the dunes or concrete steps at the beach, it sounds as if a stream rushes down behind the steps. Yet, one is only hearing the echo of the surf.

At Gnadenwald in Tyrol (Austria) is a mountain valley with soft green slopes. Only one rocky peak with barren walls protrudes. If a gun is fired in the valley, one can hear the sound of the shot roll along this wall. Each surface of the wall that is directed toward us booms the sound back with great conviction. Because all these surfaces act in sequence, the total effect resembles the roll of a thunderclap.

If one stands in an open space in the middle of a city and listens to a cannon shot, one can notice the sound rolling away into the distance until it dies away. In this case, too, house after house gives its answer.

Once I was in a forest of very tall pines. Suddenly it was as if the forest resounded with mighty bell ringing; a (propeller) airplane flew over and its rough sound seemed to turn into mellow bell ringing in the midst of these heavy pine trunks. Later, after I had lived among the trees for a long time, I noticed that one can hear the echo of each trunk separately. I experimented with many sounds of my own and also noticed an especially clear effect with the barking of dogs. Every sound that entered the forest evoked answers in all trunks, so that for a moment the whole forest sounded and resounded.

Miraculous as all these phenomena are, it should be understood that echo is based on a natural antipathy. One only finds it in bodies that refuse to assimilate and carry the sound.

If we send out a call it may echo back from all sides. This shows us that there must be something that carefully carries along our voice and spreads it further and further. One could also say that an *image* of our voice is being carried in all directions and can be echoed back to us.

If resistance occurs on this path of progress, the sound-carrying medium shrinks back in fear, as it were, and sends the sound back in another direction, often in the directly opposite direction. For a moment we might compare this to light phenomena. In a mirror we see an image of an object. Similarly, through the echo we can hear a kind of image of the source of sound. With light, as with sound, we find that the source spreads its images in all directions. But here everything happens almost instantaneously. There is no time element involved in the spreading of light as there is with the echo effect.

11

Sound Transmission Through Air

How does it happen that the sound of our voice and of every other source is carried far into the surroundings? The air that envelops and surrounds all things on the earth fully shares in every event. By itself it has no solid shape as the solid objects do. Because of that, it can intimately envelop all things. Air does not reject anything; it yields to every form; it moves with everything in motion.

When configurations actually occur in the air, they are always caused by influences that come from the outside. Most air configurations are imitations of events. The air transfers these events to the environment in their original, untouched state. What lives in the air can only be compared to a high degree of sympathy, a perfect sympathy.

When air has been eliminated in some way, sound can hardly reach our ears. Science teachers often demonstrate to their students what happens when the air around a ringing bell, which is placed under a glass dome, is slowly pumped out. The sound becomes weaker and weaker until it finally dies completely. One thing has to be carefully observed: the bell may not touch anything hard. Otherwise, sound will be transmitted through those hard solids.

If a sound is produced somewhere – in other words, if in a vibrating body a struggle exists between formative force and mass – the air so completely shares this event that it will imitate this struggle. It can only do this by creating in itself configurations in which the same relation exists between formative force and mass as in the sound producer.

These configurations are usually called *sound waves*. Low tones result in long waves, high tones in short waves. This is strikingly similar to the phenomenon that large bodies produce low tones and small bodies high ones. This phenomenon will be further explored later on.

Now we have to investigate more exactly how vibrations are transferred to the air. We will start with a vibrating tuning fork and slowly think through the events as if we were seeing them in a slow-motion movie. One moment, the prong of a tuning fork moves to the right and compresses the air ahead of it by its movement. Then, the movement is reversed, and the air behind the moving prong is, as it were, pulled apart, thinned out, rarefied.

The air has the tendency to equalize all differentiations within it by immediate redistribution of its substance. The wind is a large-scale example. It moves from places with higher barometric pressure to places with lower pressure. On a small scale, we owe to this principle the possibility of blowing or fanning the air. As soon as we compress the air in a certain place, the compression tends to spread itself in the environment.

In the case of the tuning fork, each compression immediately spreads itself over the surrounding air. This air, in its turn, transfers the push to further outlying air, etc. A push on the air, then, results in a compression that runs away farther and farther from its origin. On this course the compression gradually loses its intensity. The same description holds for the wave of rarefied air. Here more air is needed to be supplied by the immediate environment, etc.

A vibrating tuning fork thus sends out in rapid succession compressed and rarefied waves of air that spread themselves as ever-growing spheric surfaces. The official names for these waves are *condensations* and *rarefactions*.

In its laws, this phenomenon of spreading sound waves can be compared with water waves. Here, the waves give an up-and-down motion to the water particles while the waves spread horizontally: the rhythmic and the travelling motions of the water wave are at right angles. These are called *transverse waves*. With sound the rhythmic motion is back and forth, in the direction of the travelling wave. One calls *these longitudinal waves*.

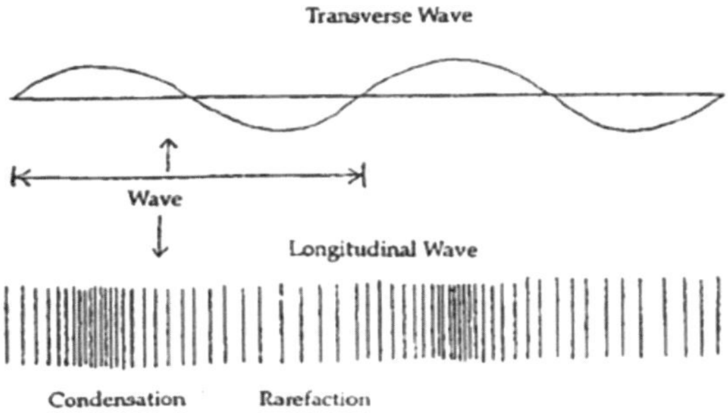

Figure 2

To put it in an image form: a sliding snake shows a kind of transversal wave; the earthworm with its elongations and contractions, a kind of longitudinal wave. In these examples one should not take into account the movements in regard to the environment.

As we have always noticed a certain relation between form and tone, there is every reason to speak also of form with regard to sound waves in the air. With a solid body, the form is mostly determined by its border with the environment. Outside the form is the environment; inside it, solid matter. With the air the form exists in variations in density. Such forms have a flowing quality, though they are concrete and can be exactly described.

These air configurations come into existence through a form disturbance of the sound-producing body. One might have called the resulting zone of dense air or the next rarefied zone one form, but it is the custom to call one condensation and one rarefaction a wave. We can also call this an *air form*.

Such forms are not tied to a certain part of the airy substance, but they run along with rushing speed and compel ever new parcels of air matter to take on their configuration. The resistance of the air that wants to eliminate each differentiation provides the motive force propelling the air forms.

There is a basic difference between the sound waves and the sound-producing body. The latter's material substance and form are in rhythmical motion. The air configurations have no substance, as we saw, and no rhythmic motion. They have a form that speeds along and gradually fades. Yet, one finds in the air also a rhythmic motion, but this one consists in the continual sequence of forms that pass by a certain spot in the air. Around the sound-producing body one finds everywhere a back-and-forth motion of the air, accompanied by rhythmic variations in pressure.

The physicist says that the lower tones have a longer wavelength and the higher tones a shorter wavelength. After what we discussed, we can now fully understand this. A body that has a high tone sends out small air configuration, a body with a lower tone, larger ones. We have seen that the basis is always a certain relation between formative force and mass. In the air the formative force is the tendency to even out any differences in pressure. This tendency is equally strong everywhere; therefore, the only way in which the relation between formative force and mass can be changed is by changing the amount of mass in each wave: we get smaller or larger forms.

12

Form Play as Window for Sounds

As soon as a tone sounds somewhere, a great playing of forms begins and penetrates into all the surroundings. By this play, the otherwise dreary, dull, inert environment becomes as it were transparent. It is as if sound from non-spatial realms shines through a window into the world of space. All bodies which hide the same tone, which have the same relation between formative force and mass as the sound maker, now resonate. The air responds to all sounds that are made. All of the air becomes transparent for sound.

13

Matter and Form as All-Encompassing Polarity

As soon as we penetrate to the core of a realm of study and clearly describe its basic law, we have built a gate through which we can find the way to the core of other, often wider, realms.

The contrast between matter and form can be found everywhere in nature.

Let us start by placing a growing plant before us. We shall be guided by Goethe's studies of metamorphosis. When the seed germinates, we first see the development of the seed leaves which "are filled as it were with raw material." (Goethe, *Metamorphosis of Plants*) With every higher row of leaves we can see more form and less substance. Finally, in the flower we hardly find any heavy matter but a remarkable wealth of forms.

Now let us consider the human figure. In the limbs and the digestive organs one finds movement connected with an intensive interchange with the surrounding material world. One finds in this realm few definite frozen forms.

However, we carry our head so that it keeps as much distance as possible from the realm of matter and heaviness. The head is solidified for the main part to one, highly differentiated form. Among the animals we find the transformation from caterpillar to butterfly: from a gluttonous and somewhat clumsy and heavy creature to an extraordinary light and delicate being which just touches the world of matter once in a while.

We can also contrast groups of animals like the bovines and the birds. Time and again we discover how these phenomena exist between the polarity of matter and form. If we penetrate deeper into the essence of this polarity we find that, through matter, phenomena are linked to forces from the depths of the earth, through form, with forces from above, from the world circumference. We can only hint at these things here as they belong in another area.

14

Matter and Form in Human Life

In Friedrich Schiller's *On the Aesthetic Education of Man*, the words *Stofftrieb* (drive towards matter) and *Formtrieb* (drive towards form) occur in an endeavor to illuminate human behavior in such a way that roads are built toward a higher form of humanity. *Stofftrieb* and *Formtrieb*, in turn, threaten to gain the upper hand. If a person is guided too much by feelings and impulses arising in him, or by sense impressions, the *Stofftrieb* is working too strongly. If he always immediately aims for the abstract laws which he can deduce from the phenomena, if his whole behavior is guided by strict thoughts and principles, the *Formtrieb* rules over his being.

In both cases he is unfree because he succumbs to the compulsion of his drives or to the compulsion of accepted or logically deduced thoughts. Schiller searched for the realm in which the human being could be free – he found it in art.

We approach art through our senses and yet we are in an atmosphere where everything is guided by strict principles. The *Spieltieb* (play impulse) governs this realm, bringing about an interplay between the two fundamental drives and thus raising them to a higher plane.

We have tried to say, briefly and inadequately, something that Schiller studied at length with all his enthusiasm and genius. Our only purpose is to indicate a basic relationship that one can verify in ones own studies. One might almost use Schiller's very words to explain tone and vibration in the study of sound. Here also opposite forces are at work. A third force brings them into interplay and lifts them to a higher level.

In human lives and in inanimate nature, therefore, we find similar relations and polarities, and yet there are vast differences between the two realms. In man's life *Stofftrieb* and *Formtrieb* constitute real, self-generated forces that cause or guide events. In the case of sound vibrations, however, formative force and inertia always have to be applied from the outside before they can develop their interchange.

15

Nature as *Werkwelt**

In the last-mentioned polarity between the laws of human life and those of inorganic nature a very important symptom is apparent. In the dead natural world one is faced with a totally completed process of creation. The creative forces have withdrawn their activity. What we find here has the character of a memory of events that once were actual. (See R. Steiner, *Life Between Death and Rebirth*, Chapter VIII.) And just as one cannot change the course of events that exist in memory, so it is also with the inorganic world. Events occur following strict laws, and, just as in our memory, they repeat themselves when the causative factor re-occurs.

Because of this the inorganic world lends itself splendidly to a schooling of our thinking and, consequently, to a development of a crystal-clear, transparent consciousness. When humanity turns toward the inorganic world, a process takes place for the earth that could be compared with the inner process in an older person. He looks back into his life, quietly surveying his experience, and now he can make it truly his own and turn it into a treasure of wisdom. One could look at the created inorganic world as a book in which one can read past events. A person engaged in this process will also learn to time his deeds

---

* Explanation of this term follows in this Section.

and the events that surround him to the laws of the past. His work and his endeavors will become productive and efficient.

Laws similar to those in the inorganic world also apply to other realms of nature, to the whole world we perceive through our senses, though this is less and less the case as one ascends to the higher kingdoms. Rudolf Steiner therefore calls the world we perceive through our senses the *Werkwelt* – a world that has become a piece of work. (See R. Steiner, *The Michael Mystery, letters to The Anthroposophical Society, starting October, 1923*, published now in *Leading Thoughts*)

16

Werkwelt and Principle of Inertia

Everything in the *Werkwelt* functions according to strict laws. Everything happens as it happened before. Here we find the principle of inertia in the widest possible sense. The occurrence of inertia is the result of the withdrawal of creative forces.

No real changes occur in the *Werkwelt* from within. They do take place from without. The only agent that can make such changes is the human being who is both part of the *Werkwelt* and, at the same time, carries something in himself which stands outside the *Werkwelt*.

Though earth-nature has been a *Werkwelt* for aeons, the human spirit has only recently developed the ability to accept this fully and to handle the concept in his thinking. And yet one finds countless people who consider miracles possible or who search for miracles. They unconsciously count on the interception of supernatural powers in natural events. Their belief keeps them from looking at things in a practical, business-like manner. Others try to break through the limits that nature has set for us by attending seances or pursuing other kinds of magic tricks.

It is no wonder that those who saw the true nature of things often acted aggressively and that they often went too far in their statements.

One example of this is the accepted statement of the principle of inertia: "A body cannot by itself change its state of rest or state of motion." Rudolf Steiner points out that this is not correctly stated, that it should be: "A body which by itself cannot change its state of rest or motion, we call an inorganic body." (*Truth and Science*) Maybe we might also say that we call such a body "inert."

The generally accepted statement implies that the laws of the *Werkwelt*, and actually those of inorganic nature, are the only valid ones. The second statement fully allows for the possibility that there are other realms with other laws.

Very elegant is also the statement by Leonardo: "Nothing without a mind – insensate – moves by itself; its movement is caused by others." With this belongs what Leonardo says about force, in other words, about the counterpole to inertia which continually interacts with it: "… its true origin lies in those bodies which have senses." (Marie Herzfeld, *Leonardo der Denker, Forscher und Poet*, pp. 14,17)

In reality the whole *Werkwelt*, and especially inorganic nature, can be considered a kind of excretion of the spirit. Yet, in the materialistic era one became more and more convinced that what we carry in ourselves as spirit is only a product of material processes that follow the laws of the inorganic world. Many scientific statements exemplify this.

Leonardo, one of the greatest inaugurators of the new scientific age, did not make this mistake. His statements are precise, leaving open a road to the spirit.

17

Freedom as Victory Over Inertia

Rudolf Steiner clearly showed that the human being is a creature on the road to freedom. A free act is determined only by the central essence of the acting person. No influence from outside, or from the bodily organism, must play any role. In the case of such a free deed, therefore, the principle of inertia in its widest meaning has been conquered and overthrown.

Steiner set himself the task of leading human insight and human consciousness beyond the borders of the *Werkwelt*. Many strong spirits had already tried to break through these borders before him. But he was the first one to see how even the inorganic realm is related to the spirit.

It is interesting to compare Steiner's approach with Leonardo's. Leonardo fully enters the *Werkwelt* without closing the road to the spirit. Steiner opens a new road to the spirit, making fully visible the connection with the inorganic world.

Steiner pointed toward human consciousness where the spirit can be fully free (Steiner, *Philosophy of Spiritual Activity*). An unbiased study of the *Werkwelt*, especially of the realms of nature, leads beyond its limitations (Steiner, *Goethe's World View*). One can notice in such studies a continual ascending. Inertia is gradually overcome and the phenomena more and more show their kinship with the spiritual world.

Already in the plant kingdom we find a continual self-determined transformation where the inorganic inertia (inertia in its narrow sense) is being conquered. In the animal kingdom we see a much greater variability and mobility which is determined by a non-material soul-world. Yet, even here, all of animal life is a repetition of the same program. Everything is determined from the past. An animal seems to understand only the situation in which it acts. In reality, an animal's actions can be compared with those of a person who long ago understood something that he now has forgotten. This person's actions are a complete repetition of what he once decided to do. The animal is totally locked into the past; it belongs to the *Werkwelt*.

Only the human being rises above the *Werkwelt*. Only with him do we find a consciousness that lives completely in the present. Only man can be the first cause in a series of events because he can choose not to be determined by the past. He can fully see through a situation he faces and then initiate new events. Here he is not a creature – a product, a piece of work – but a creator. In his hands rests the task to continue the creation. When he acts freely, he opens a window in the *Werkwelt* through which the light of the spirit can shine in. Only man can be a "prime mover"; only he can relate his deeds to the future.

As we discussed in section 16, spiritual beings long ago withdrew their activity from the *Werkwelt*. Now, however, when man elevates himself to the realization of freedom, spirit can again enter the *Werkweltt* and inertia can be overcome.

18

Nature Lost Its Sound

By such considerations we can begin to understand something Rudolf Steiner pointed out. The further one goes back in world history, the more the man of that time perceived the world as permeated with sound. In the Lemurian man, for example, this was caused by his greater capacity to reach into supersensible realms than in modern man. In *Cosmic Memory*, Steiner writes with regard to the female leaders in late Lemurian times:

> In certain higher dreams the secrets of nature were divulged to them and they received the impulses for their actions. Everything was animated for them and showed itself to them in soul powers and apparitions. They abandoned themselves to the mysterious weaving of their soul forces. That which impelled them to their actions were "inner voices," or what

plants, animals, stones, wind and clouds, the whispering of the trees and so on told them.

In the earliest periods of time, however, the total environment of man was so completely filled with and penetrated by life, soul and spirit that there was no separation between sensible and supersensible. Sound did not arise as a result of external forces as is the case in our time. Sound came forth from the inside of everything that surrounded man. Rudolf Steiner says:

> For what man perceives at this stage through his connection with the Earth does not consist of so many physical objects. He lives in the sensations of warmth that rise up to him, and in sounds, and within these streams of warmth and surging waves of sound he feels the presence of the Spirits of Personality and the Archangels. (*Occult Science – an Outline*)

In our time nature has become a finished piece of work, completed by the spiritual beings who created it. Earlier nature was more a tool or even the body of those spiritual beings. Initially it was not even possible to distinguish the spiritual beings from their creations. If one goes back this far, one stands in a world consisting of god-like beings whose deeds can be heard as sounds. The interaction of these deeds are expressed in harmonies. These beings express their essence in archetypal words ("In the beginning was the Word...").

If one searches carefully, one finds traces of knowledge of these conditions in our folklore. More rarely one finds persons in whom some memory of former conditions seems to exist. For example, Novalis, in *Die Lehrlinge*, speaks of "the hushed and lost sounds in the air and the woods." (*Die verstummten und verlornen Tone in Luft and Waeldern.*)

In fairy tales there are often references to a time when animals were still able to speak. In other lore one finds similar indications that once the water or the air had voices. The heavenly bodies occur as personalities with whom discussions are possible. Richard Wagner saw musical instruments as images of archetypal powers of creation.

19

Ascending to Realms of Sound and Word

Not only in the distant past do we find worlds that are filled with sound. Rudolf Steiner points out that if one can free one's consciousness of its connection with the *Werkwelt*, one can ascend to worlds that express themselves, even in our present time, in sound and tone. This can be accomplished by inner development. (See, for example, Steiner's *Knowledge of the Higher Worlds and Its Attainment.*)

Such a development has many aspects. One very important element is that one loosens ones connection with physical matter and, consequently, overcomes the rigidity in one's own being. The physical world is especially characterized by inertia and impenetrability. The latter principle can be expressed in this way: "Where one body exists, another one cannot be." Especially solid bodies, therefore, are completely separated from each other and, because of their rigid form, confined within specific borders. To the degree that we are concentrated on ourselves and thus isolated from other beings, to that degree, we contribute to impenetrability. To the extent that we allow the contents of our consciousness and of our actions to be determined from the outside, we participate in inertia.

These two characteristics especially show our connection with physical matter and with the *Werkwelt*. Therefore, first of all, we have to free ourselves from heaviness and inertia. Then we slowly learn to raise ourselves to higher realms. One might also say that within us new worlds emerge.

But we also have to learn to free ourselves of the consequences of impenetrability, of the rigid form of our own being, so that we gain the ability to understand other beings so completely that we, as it were, become one with them.

We can search, therefore, for realms of sound and tone in the distant past, before nature was frozen in its form and when the inertia of matter had not yet thrown a veil over spiritual activity, or we can aspire toward realms that exist far above matter and rigid form.

20

Realms of Word and Sound; Mirrored in the Physical World

The term harmony of the spheres has often been used. To a consciousness that has risen above earthbound experiences, the universe is filled with mighty, harmonious sound expressions.

The planets express their being and the relations between them not only in movement but also in melody, rhythm and harmony. One of the last ones who still received impressions from this realm was Goethe. He describes this in exact terms in his *Faust*:

The day-star, sonorous as of old,
Goes his predestined way along,
And round his path is thunder rolled
While sister-spheres join rival song.

Prologue in Heaven

Hark! The Hours, with furious winging,
Bear to spirit-ears the ringing
Rumour of the new day springing
Gates of rock grind back asunder,
Phoebus comes with wheels of thunder:
Light spreads tumult through the air.

Loud are trump and timbrel sounded,
Eyes are dazed and ears astounded,
Sounds unheard of none may bear.

Act 1, Scene 1, Part It

In one's inward journey, one has to ascend to a still higher sphere – to the fixed stars, to the zodiac – to approach the realm of the "cosmic word."

From these realms of sound and word comes everything that surrounds us. At one time there was only a world of sound and tone and the mighty power of the Word. Gradually our present world separated itself from this realm. Sound became hushed but left an impression of its being in cosmic relationships and in the laws that determine world events. One might say, therefore, that nature is congealed sound. For a long time many people still had the gift of raising themselves to experience the source of nature in sound. Ultimately, not only did this sound die; humanity lost the inner capacity to hear.

Through these events modern human consciousness is imprisoned in the *Werkwelt* as if it were locked up in a soundproof box. We have become strangers in the realm where we belong.

Yet sound can penetrate into our world. Not only some splinters and broken pieces but even pure images of events in the super-spatial world of sound can be heard with our physical ears. If we want this to happen, we have to bring about a movement, an imbalance, in a material substance. And the material has to be set up in such a way that it answers with a strict rhythmical vibration. What is the essence of such a rhythm? It is a counter image of cosmic events.

If we study the movements of sun, moon and planets as they appear to our eyes, we come to see that they are based on an interplay of oscillations that follow the same laws as the oscillations and vibrations in our surroundings. (See Baravalle, *Die Erscheinungen am Sternenhimmel*.)

We can produce pure tones by creating conditions in physical matter that mirror the events in the spheres of the planets. For the pitch of a tone one has to aim for a specific relation between mass and formative force. To create the needed volume and tone character one usually needs to build a resonating space that is based on strictly defined proportions of form. I do not have any doubt that these laws also will be found to mirror cosmic constellations.

Rudolf Steiner says in his first natural science course, *The Light Course:* *

> Essentially, sound waves in the air are related to a tone only in as far as they create a suction process where the tone is drawn in from non-spatial realms.

Now it can become clear, from a new aspect, why inorganic nature so rarely produces pure tones and never, under any circumstances, music. Steiner speaks of matter as a "*Truemmerhaufen des Geistes*" – a "heap of spirit-debris." (*The World of the Senses and the World of the Spirit*) Matter has, as it were, tumbled down from the sphere of spiritual law and spiritual form-principles. In the crystals the spiritual principles of form have been preserved in frozen form.

The image given earlier comparing a pure tone in the midst of a world of noise with a crystal within a mass of stone has found new validity.

Only by raising matter to a higher level and linking it to specific laws of form can the pure tone, and ultimately instrumental music, be produced.

In the "cosmic word" the highest forces from realms of stars express themselves. In it sounds the origin of things.

This represents still higher laws than the musical ones. Rudolf Steiner says:

---

* Ten lectures given in Stuttgart, Dec. 23,1919, to Jan. 3,1920. Now available in publication from Rudolf Steiner Schools Fellowship.

> And as today we men clothe words in tones, so in times past did the divine Word of the Worlds clothe itself in the music of the spheres.... And, as today man compels the air into forms with his word and his singing and his tone, so did the divine words and the divine music bring forth forms. (*The World of the Senses and the World of the Spirit*)

Earlier we saw that the air movements that sound makes – the sound waves – should be considered as forms. Speech also brings the air into forms like those made by pure tones. But another form principle plays a role here. The sound-flow itself receives form. If one holds one's fingers in front of the mouth while speaking specific sounds with real emphasis, especially consonants, one can notice some of these characteristic forms. Certainly, other means can be found to make these forms visible.

This description of the formative power of the word is in accordance with Steiner's quotation regarding the relationship between the music of the spheres and the word of God. It is important here to notice that the word is completely tied to the living organs of speech of the human being while music can also be produced on instruments.

Leaving aside human speech and manmade instruments, we want to give you this image of nature untouched by man: in the beginning the whole world was filled with sound and word-power. Slowly, nature began to congeal and to fall silent. Many sounds remained in the world but they did not speak or sing any longer of the archetypal creative powers. The word and music withdrew from the environment and remained only as a gift of the human being. But here and there, for example in bird song, we can still hear harmony and melody in nature. This is true, of course, when one hears a single bird. However, on a country walk, just before sunrise on a spring morning, one may feel oneself carried by an ocean of sublime sound created by all the birds.

21

About Emergence of Word Power, About Its Loss

Rudolf Steiner describes the moment in man's development – late Lemuria, early Atlantis. (See *Cosmic Memory*.) – where man received the power of the word and with this a great power over his fellow beings and over nature.

Steiner says, speaking about the Rmoahals, the first Atlantic race:

> The soul powers of these fast Atlanteans still possessed something of the forces of nature.... Their soul powers were more connected with forces of nature than are those of modern man. Thus the speech-word which they produced had something of the power of nature. They not only *named* things but in their words was a *power* over things and also over their fellow men.... When a Rmoahals man pronounced a word, this word developed a power similar to that of the object it designated. Because of this, words at that time were curative; they could advance the growth of plants, tame the rage of animals and perform other similar functions. All this progressively decreased in force among the later sub-races of the Atlanteans. One could say that the original fullness of power was gradually lost. The Rmoahals men felt this plenitude of power to be a gift of mighty nature, and their relationship to the latter had a religious character. For them language was something especially sacred. The misuse of certain sounds, which possessed an important power, was an impossibility.... In a kind of innocence of feeling the Rmoahals ascribed their power not so much to themselves as to the *divine nature* acting within them.
>
> (*Cosmic Memory*)

Steiner further indicates that this power decreased more and more as human beings increasingly began to feel their personal value and, accordingly, were less open to divine beings. In addition, it must have played a role that in those early times nature was more fully penetrated by life, that the minerals were less hard, so that nature was more easily influenced than in later times. Man became more and more separated from the spirit, nature congealed, became fixed in its forms and subject to inertia. The spiritual world became heavily veiled. The human voice now was tied to matter. Speech was no longer an expression of creative force, no longer radiated through by fiery, divine activity. It simply became a means of communication.

Yet, even now, sound still has power, even now, our voice can intervene in a formative manner.

22

About the Search for the Real Power of the Word

Rudolf Steiner said repeatedly that human words would gain a new power in the future. A first indication of this is the speech work which was developed according to his guidelines. Steiner pointed out that one must learn to let the spoken word be *leibfrei* (literally: *free of the body*) and, therefore, also free of the too personal element. He also gave extensive guidance on the essence of language and its sound components so that it is now possible to let the essential nature of the sounds and the words sound through. One can learn to allow spirit to work into speech again.

A second indication of the future power of the word can be found in eurythmy, the new art of movement inaugurated by Steiner. In the practice of this art, the eurythmist subjects her or himself voluntarily to the forming power of the word and of music.

If we want to go further in searching for the power of sound, and if we also want to influence processes of nature, we must connect first of all with events where rigidity and inertia hardly play a role.

In two methods of research the influence of supersensible forces has been clearly demonstrated: chromatography and crystallization. (See E. & L. Kolisko, *Agriculture of Tomorrow*, and E. Pfeiffer, *Sensitive Crystallization Processes.*) In studying these methods it is striking that the starting point for both is a fluid which then, very slowly, is allowed to take on form. The important thing here is that the form is spread out in a plane. Heaviness and inertia play almost no role in these processes. Therefore, the formative process can be sensitive to extremely subtle influences. Here we have something that runs parallel to the changes in consciousness needed in the training toward supersensible perception.

Our everyday consciousness, an object consciousness, is tied to three-dimensional space. The imaginative consciousness, the first higher level of consciousness that lifts itself to the supersensible, frees itself of three-dimensional space and enters a two-dimensional realm.

It is quite understandable that scientific experiments have generally taken place in three-dimensional space. By arranging an experiment so that the third dimension is excluded, the results can contain valuable images. Similarly, the images appearing in imaginative consciousness can be a mirror of supersensible events.

Rudolf Steiner once pointed out that for research involving sound and spoken word, the sensitive flame of Tyndall should be used*.

In this example also we have an extremely mobile research material which is hardly subject to rigidity and inertia. (Also

---

* **Translator's note**: In Tyndall's book, *Sound*, this flame is described as a special 18-inch-tall gas flame that is so sensitive that it responds to different vowels by drastically changing its height. Tyndall calls it the "vowel flame." He recited poetry to this flame and describes the resulting dance of the flame.

compare P. E. Schiller: *Untersuchungen an der freien schallempfindlichen Flamme, Akustische Zeitschrift 3*).

23

Word Power and Conquering of *Werkwelt*

When we accomplish a rekindling of a spiritual fire in the human voice and when we are able to find nature processes which are almost free of the power of mass and rigid form, then we are winning back something that was given to us in the earliest times; however, at that time these were divine powers that worked directly in the world. Now the human being has to raise himself to the true essence of things and give voice to this essence. The creative forces no longer speak through him; he himself will have to let the essence speak. Yes, he can empower the supersensible so that it can initiate new creation processes. The snake promised man that he would become like a god if he ate of the tree of knowledge. The fruit of this tree gave him the ability to think independently and therefore to err, but it also gave him the ability to rise to the highest insights. And Rudolf Steiner adds to this that man can thank Lucifer (i.e. the snake) for the gift of the word:

> ... but the rest of mankind also received special faculties through the working of the Luciferian principle, inasmuch as the great cosmic Beings turned to good what might otherwise have been quite detrimental. One such faculty is that of speech. *(Occult Science – an Outline)*

Therefore, man has become a being who is on the way to developing god-like powers. He has received a seed which, when he learns to let it grow, will develop into the highest powers of creation.

The divine powers have withdrawn from the *Werkwelt*, leaving man in deep loneliness. The *Werkwelt* is lost for further development if man does not reintroduce there the divine, reconnecting it with the original, archetypal creative forces. Thus man can further the world as he ascends in his own development. All this can only be accomplished because the divine word has become flesh in Jesus Christ. He testifies: "I have conquered the world." What once was achieved by one human being – that he raised himself so high that the highest divine power could descend – that is the archetypal image for human life.

Christ is the conqueror of the *Werkwelt*. This seems to have been the great problem with which Leonardo wrestled when he was painting *The Last Supper*. How could he paint, respecting natures laws in his use of light, and yet paint Christ's figure so that it radiated light? In his science Leonardo left open the road to the spirit. In his art he already searched for a new road to the spirit.

So Christ is the true conveyor of freedom. Human beings, because they live in the *Werkwelt*, have been torn away from the divine world. Thanks to the Mystery of Golgotha, man can again reconnect himself with the divine powers and with their help free himself from the restraints of the *Werkwelt*. He can, with ceaseless effort, develop not only his soul but also his body to bring them closer to the divine.

Christ has renewed the word. When He spoke, great powers worked through His voice. We know from the Gospels that His words had a tremendous effect on His listeners.

24

Lines of Development in the Area of Sound Production

At the same time that humanity began to develop technology, we see a grand development of instrumental music and particularly of the orchestra. The orchestra offers awe-inspiring possibilities. Thanks to the quality of the instruments and the skills and good will of the players, the conductor stands there like a being with godlike power and authority, transforming into living sound what lives inside him.

Though the instruments have been constructed from dead materials in the *Werkwelt*, the confinements of the *Werkwelt* are transcended when the orchestra plays. Though the instruments obey physical laws, they mirror at the same time high creative powers.

When an orchestra plays, heaviness, inertia and especially fixedness have no power. The sound has freed itself to a very high degree from its material bonds and it can rise to heavenly spheres. Exalted powers can then descend and work on man's inner nature. In such music one can find an image of what happens in the sphere of creation. (See R. Steiner, *The Arts and Their Mission.*)

From these considerations it becomes clear that we can speak of true music only when the instrument is built in such a way and the playing is done so that the sound can free itself from its material bonds.

What do we see, however? There are more and more forms of sound production where just these material bonds are emphasized. An example of this is jazz. All the elements that should be conquered in music – the accompanying noises and distorted sounds caused by the instrument's material nature: the mechanical element in the rhythm that is an expression of inertia, etc. – are accentuated. In the area of sound this is an expression of satisfaction that we here in the *Werkwelt* are cut off from the divine. Jazz wants nothing to do with our yearning for spiritual freedom and redemption from material bonds.

There are mechanical sound-producing devices whose construction can be said to be based on a degeneration of thinking. The simplest of these is the siren. Its design is based on the following thought process: "Sound is nothing else but a vibration of the air. Therefore, if we can get the air to vibrate in some manner we shall get sound." The result which we all have experienced, often painfully, confirms the correctness of the thoughts, but only for those who lack an organ for perceiving the higher nature that can live in sound. Instead of a rhythm in which divine powers live, we have here a purely mechanical sequence of air thrusts. I understand that efforts have even been made to elevate the siren to a musical instrument.

But not only the sounds of instruments, the human voice also can be wrested from its origin and mechanically controlled. Our world is full of mechanical voice-reproducing devices. They are based on this thought sequence: "The voice causes vibrations and forms in the air of which an imprint can be made in some kind of medium. When this imprint is again transformed to air vibrations we regain the sound of the voice."

If one hears a real voice, if one hears true music, one can immerse oneself in the sound without reservation, and, helped by regular practice, penetrate deeper into hidden realities that are expressed in this sound. If one does this with a siren, one can only experience a soulless and even a soul-destroying activity.

25

About the Powers Fighting for the Word

Humanity stands before the task to bring the divine again into the *Werkwelt*. We see that the true artist uses his material, his sounds, so that the divine helps to form and build his images and his sound structures. We see him elevate his material so far that a glow of heaven shines or sounds in it. He disengages his work from the laws of the *Werkwelt* and makes it obey higher laws.

The technician works with the *Werkwelt* in a different way. He brings about a very fundamental conversion and transformation of matter. In technology we really have a realized thought world or, rather, a realized world of ideas. A technology is conceivable which would be in the service of the divine and of the wholesome development of man, and there even are tender sprouts of inventions that go in this direction. If we really want to follow this road it will before all else be necessary to remove self-interest from the current work methods and machines. But even the thoughts behind new inventions will have to take on other forms.

We can get an inkling of other possibilities when we hear from Rudolf Steiner that a technology will dawn where the power of the word will play a special role. This points towards a technology that is deeply connected with the human being, that does not confront him as an icy-cold, alien power. Yes, even high moral development will play a role here. Imagine a situation where a kind of factory can be set in motion by the word or words of a certain individual, and this only because this person has reached a certain moral level.

Here we stand before a new form of the power of the word. This will also become a road toward an ever deeper influence of the Christ-power on the *Werkwelt*. The persons who will guide this technology will only be able to work in a healing way if they practice the words of Paul in deep earnestness: "Not I – Christ in me."

One can see how important this ideal is when one considers the negative counterimages. As we saw, scientists are continually busy to master the human voice and to separate it from the human being. There is arguably nothing more characteristic of our time than that we have speaking machines.

There is a fierce battle around the human word. To the degree that this divine gift becomes mechanized and tied to matter will the events in the *Werkwelt* become more and more cut off from their source. On the opposite side, the highest ideal lights up before us as a beacon: to raise the word to its divine origin. Of course, art will have to play a leading role in this process. How else could the voice be developed, how else could we free ourselves from every-day banality, than by raising ourselves in the practice of real art? But such practice brings the danger that we separate ourselves proudly in our ivory tower – that we do not transform ourselves into true servants of Christ.

No, self-improvement is not the only task of the renewed word. It will have to heal and it will have to penetrate into the technology, into the processes of nature.

It will be as a light that shines into the darkness.

Appendix

One of the most exciting, surprising and inspiring demonstrations in the area of sound and tone is the Chladni plate. (Chladni was a French scientist in the early nineteenth century.) Fine sand or salt is sprinkled on top of a metal plate that is supported in the center. The edge of the plate is bowed until a steady pitch is obtained. The vibration of the plate arranges the particles into a sharply defined, symmetrical pattern. The higher the pitch, the more intricate and complex is the pattern.

Frits Julius compares a pure tone in the world of sound with a crystal in the world of minerals. Only a pure tone will call forth a sharply defined form on a Chladni plate. To me, such a Chladni pattern is like a beautiful crystal. What brings the experience beyond that of watching a crystal is that one is present at the moment of birth.

If your interest in the world of sound has increased after reading *Sound Between Matter and Spirit*, and if you have never seen a Chladni demonstration, you owe it to yourself to correct this deficiency. No children should grow up without experiencing the Chladni plate, but relatively few students outside Waldorf Schools see it.

Many science museums and children's museums nowadays have a Chladni plate but very often not in good working order. It is not sufficient to see the particles vibrate and take on some vague form That could be compared with watching a crystal through clouded glasses. Try contacting a Waldorf School if your efforts have failed elsewhere.

The twenty-five brief sections of *Sound Between Matter and Spirit* are written with great economy. I have always felt that Frits Julius would have given considerable attention to the Chladni plate if he had ever written an expanded version of his book. That is the reason I have added this appendix. More information on the Chladni plate is included in the following article. The article was originally written in 1968, which dates some of the information given.

The Chladni Plate – Meeting Point of Two Worlds *

Waldorf students have their first acquaintance with physics in the sixth grade. Worlds of wonder open, up: light and dark give birth to sparkling colors that mix in surprising ways (Did you know that red and green could make yellow?); a hot-air balloon rises slowly and majestically, a flame dances and quivers, sensitive to sounds we make.

One of the most fascinating experiences in acoustics is the demonstration of Chladni's plate. This is a simple metal plate, usually circular or square, supported in the center. Fine sand or salt is sprinkled on top. The edge is bowed with a violin bow, and, with some skill and luck, one can induce the plate to sing a pure note. Behold! The grains of sand suddenly arrange themselves in a sharply defined, symmetrical pattern.

With one magic stroke, intricate and beautiful order is created from chaos. The suddenness of this event is a never-ending source of wonder for the children They hold their breath when the bow is applied to the plate, and, if the stroke is successful, they respond with a most heartfelt "Aahh!"

A particular Chladni plate can be made to vibrate at dozens of different pitches, each one commanding its own form. The higher the pitch, the more intricate the pattern becomes. By applying dry ice or vibrating piezoelectric crystals to the plate, one can produce notes of very high frequencies, resulting in patterns of astonishing variety, detail and beauty. The two illustrations show simple patterns on a round and on a square plate. The first form was obtained by bowing the edge, the second one by touching the square plate with a chip of dry ice.

---

* Originally published in *Education as an Art*, Summer, 1968.

After Chladni's work around 1800, little research was done until recent times. The latest work is connected with the names of Mary Waller, formerly physicist at the London School of Medicine, and Hans Jenny, medical doctor of Dornach, Switzerland. The latter, in cooperation with a photographer, an actor and a Waldorf teacher, produced a motion picture, *Vibrating World*, which was shown on television in Germany and now travels through the United States as part of an art exhibit sponsored by International Business Machines.

It is hard to describe the fascination of watching the creative moment on a Chladni plate. After the tone dies out, the pattern on the plate remains and can be admired and studied. Yet this is a postmortem – one is looking at a corpse. The living drama unrolls when the sounding tone, as a dance master, conducts the dancing particles to their places in a splendid choreography.

Sometimes one may produce a note with wavering pitch. It is then as if two or more dance masters were giving conflicting orders. There is a struggle between the forms, they change back and forth, and one waits with bated breath to see which will win.

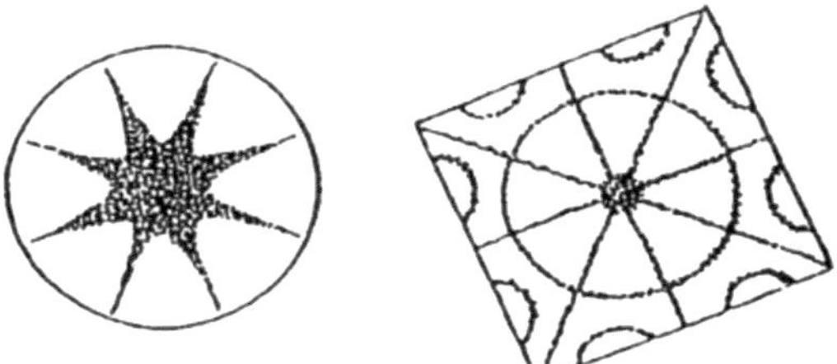

Forms on Chladni plates

Figure 3

The Chladni plate is a meeting point of two worlds. Material and non-material worlds meet, and it is the not-visible that shapes the visible. Spenser wrote:

For of the soul the body form doth take;
For soul is form, and doth the body make

Emerson said: "Nature is the incarnation of a thought, and turns to a thought again, as ice becomes water and gas. The world is mind precipitated…"

We all experience that a person's face is an expression of, is shaped by, his own unique spirit. The Chladni plate shows that each tone also has its own physiognomy. If a simple, mechanically produced tone has such an intricately beautiful shaping force, the human voice must introduce a still higher order of form-giving. The brand-new invention of *voice prints*, as unique for one individual as his fingerprints, may possibly demonstrate one aspect of this realm. Yet, with all of these phenomena, we are only in the foothills of this landscape. In the background towers the archetype of all shaping forces, as voiced by St. John: "In the beginning [of all things] was the [creative] Word...."

– Gerhard Bedding

In the feeling we have today when we hear the word "Word" there remains nothing at all of what the writer of the Gospel of St. John felt when he wrote "In the beginning was the Word." ... To the Greeks the word was still a call to the human will. When a syllable was uttered, the body of a Greek would tingle to express this syllable through his whole being also.... The word did not only live in the organ of speech but in the whole of man's organism of movement.

There was a tingling, an urge in the human being to let the will reveal itself through the limbs, with every syllable, with every word, with the rhythm and measure of every phrase. He realized how the world could become creative in every movement. But in those days he knew still more. Words were to him expressions for the forces of cloud formation, the forces lying in the growth of plants and all natural phenomena. The word rumbled in the rolling waves, worked in the whistling wind. Just as the word lives in my breath so that I make a corresponding movement, so did the Greek find all that was living in the word in the raging wind, in the surging wave, even in the rumbling earthquake. These were words pouring out of the earth.

– Rudolf Steiner
From *Education and Modern Spiritual Life*
Twelve lectures,
Ilkley, England, 1923